WITHDRAWAL

The Black Death

The Black Death

Tracee de Hahn

CHELSEA HOUSE PUBLISHERS
Philadelphia

Frontispiece: A 19th-century artist captured the terror associated with the medieval plague in a painting depicting a nighttime visit from the Angel of Death.

CHELSEA HOUSE PUBLISHERS

Editor in Chief Sally Cheney
Director of Production Kim Shinners
Production Manager Pamela Loos
Art Director Sara Davis
Production Editor Diann Grasse

Staff for THE BLACK DEATH

Senior Editor John Ziff
Associate Editor J. Christopher Higgins
Layout 21st Century Publishing and Communications, Inc.

First Printing

1 3 5 7 9 8 6 4 2

The Chelsea House World Wide Web address is
http://www.chelseahouse.com

Library of Congress Cataloging-in-Publication Data

De Hahn, Tracee.
    The Black death / Tracee De Hahn.
        p. cm. — (Great disasters)
    Includes bibliographical references and index.
    Summary: Describes the origins, spread, and effects of the terrible plague that devastated fourteenth-century Europe.
    ISBN 0-7910-6326-7 (alk. paper)
    1. Black death—History—Juvenile literature. 2. Medicine, Medieval—Juvenile Literature. [1. Black death—History. 2. Plague—History. 3. Diseases—History.] I. Title. II. Series.

RC172.D425 2001
616.9'232—dc21   2001032491

Contents

GREAT DISASTERS
REFORMS and RAMIFICATIONS

Jill McCaffrey
National Chairman
Armed Forces Emergency Services
American Red Cross

Introduction

Disasters have always been a source of fascination and awe. Tales of a great flood that nearly wipes out all life are among humanity's oldest recorded stories, dating at least from the second millennium B.C., and they appear in cultures from the Middle East to the Arctic Circle to the southernmost tip of South America and the islands of Polynesia. Typically gods are at the center of these ancient disaster tales—which is perhaps not too surprising, given the fact that the tales originated during a time when human beings were at the mercy of natural forces they did not understand.

To a great extent, we still are at the mercy of nature, as anyone who reads the newspapers or watches nightly news broadcasts can attest.

Hurricanes, earthquakes, tornados, wildfires, and floods continue to exact a heavy toll in suffering and death, despite our considerable knowledge of the workings of the physical world. If science has offered only limited protection from the consequences of natural disasters, it has in no way diminished our fascination with them. Perhaps that's because the scale and power of natural disasters force us as individuals to confront our relatively insignificant place in the physical world and remind us of the fragility and transience of our lives. Perhaps it's because we can imagine ourselves in the midst of dire circumstances and wonder how we would respond. Perhaps it's because disasters seem to bring out the best and worst instincts of humanity: altruism and selfishness, courage and cowardice, generosity and greed.

As one of the national chairmen of the American Red Cross, a humanitarian organization that provides relief for victims of disasters, I have had the privilege of seeing some of humanity's best instincts. I have witnessed communities pulling together in the face of trauma; I have seen thousands of people answer the call to help total strangers in their time of need.

Of course, helping victims after a tragedy is not the only way, or even the best way, to deal with disaster. In many cases planning and preparation can minimize damage and loss of life—or even avoid a disaster entirely. For, as history repeatedly shows, many disasters are caused not by nature but by human folly, shortsightedness, and unethical conduct. For example, when a land developer wanted to create a lake for his exclusive resort club in Pennsylvania's Allegheny Mountains in 1880, he ignored expert warnings and cut corners in reconstructing an earthen dam. On May 31, 1889, the dam gave way, unleashing 20 million tons of water on the towns below. The Johnstown Flood, the deadliest in American history, claimed more than 2,200 lives. Greed and negligence would figure prominently in the Triangle Shirtwaist Company fire in 1911. Deplorable conditions in the garment sweatshop, along with a failure to give any thought to the safety of workers, led to the tragic deaths of 146 persons. Technology outstripped wisdom only a year later, when the designers of the luxury liner *Titanic* smugly declared their state-of-the-art ship "unsinkable," seeing no need to provide lifeboat capacity for everyone onboard. On the night of April 14, 1912, more than 1,500 passengers and crew paid for this hubris with their lives after the ship collided with an iceberg and sank. But human catastrophes aren't always the unforeseen consequences of carelessness or folly. In the 1940s the leaders of Nazi Germany purposefully and systematically set out to exterminate all Jews, along with Gypsies, homosexuals, the mentally ill, and other so-called undesirables. More recently terrorists have targeted random members of society, blowing up airplanes and buildings in an effort to advance their political agendas.

The books in the GREAT DISASTERS: REFORMS AND RAMIFICATIONS series examine these and other famous disasters, natural and human made. They explain the causes of the disasters, describe in detail how events unfolded, and paint vivid portraits of the people caught up in dangerous circumstances. But these books are more than just accounts of what happened to whom and why. For they place the disasters in historical perspective, showing how people's attitudes and actions changed and detailing the steps society took in the wake of each calamity. And in the end, the most important lesson we can learn from any disaster—as well as the most fitting tribute to those who suffered and died—is how to avoid a repeat in the future.

A wood carving on the wall of a French plague ossuary, or repository for the bones of the dead. Between 1347 and 1351, the Black Death ravaged Europe, killing one-third to one-half of the population.

A New Kind of Fear

A group of men and women wearing masks, gloves, surgical scrubs, and eye protection clustered around a collection of stained bones. The bones were laid out on the table exactly as they had been found in the grave: skull, amazingly intact for its age; rib cage, collapsed but all there; spine; pelvis; arms; and legs. The average observer would not be able to deduce much about the life of the person whose skeleton now lay on the table. But for these osteologists (scientists who examine bones), forensic pathologists (scientists who examine body tissues and fluids for signs of disease), and historians, there were many clues. The length of the skeleton indicated the person's approximate age at the time of death, and the pelvic bones revealed the skeleton's sex. The scientists would rely on a thorough analysis of the ribs and teeth for a more precise age, but the group agreed that the bones were those of an adolescent boy who had died of the Black Death.

Photographs of the skeleton had been taken at the archaeological site where the bones had been found and in the laboratory. One photograph showed that a small stone scratched with a deep cross had been lying in the grave near the skeleton's hip, indicating that the stone had probably been in a pouch tied to the boy's waist. No one said anything, but all were well aware of the terrible manner of the boy's death: the fever, the delirium, the eruption of petechiae—tiny capillary hemorrhages no larger than the head of a pin, caused by overwhelming infection—and, finally, the bulging buboes (swelling of the lymph glands, usually in the area of the groin and armpits). Most likely, fear and an inability to understand why the sickness had struck had also accompanied all of these physical symptoms.

This skeleton had come from Smithfield in London, a name that had meaning especially for the historians in the group. They knew that a cemetery had been opened at Smithfield for plague victims after the huge number of dead filled London's existing cemeteries. Hurriedly consecrated by the bishop of London, Ralph Stratford, the cemetery at Smithfield had itself filled quickly and was followed by the opening of another at Spittle Croft. By examining skeletons from these and other plague cemeteries, the scientists hoped to learn more about the disease that had struck their young victim and so many others in the 14th century.

Some of the bones were selected and a fine layer of contaminated bone was ground away. The ground bone and the remaining bone would be studied; some parts would be pulverized and dissolved in solutions in an attempt to locate and study the DNA of the plague strain that caused the Black Death. (DNA, or deoxyribonucleic acid, is a complex molecule that exists in all cellular organisms and that contains the blueprint for each organism.) Many other tests would follow, since numerous scientists and historians were interested in the story of the remains. It was pure chance that led them to examine this skeleton so carefully. They had thousands to choose from, all recently excavated from the mass graves of those who had died in the plague of 1348–1350. Although the scientists would never know the names or occupations of the victims whose bones they were examining, they had other interests and questions: Why had the plague killed so many? How had it traveled? What were its different types, or strains?

What the group did know, historians had pieced together from chronicles, the written accounts left by those who had witnessed the Black Death. These chronicles were more than 600 years old. Because the disease struck in an age before the printing press, the only surviving accounts were handwritten. They were few in number, and sometimes suspect because the sheer terror of the disease probably led survivors to exaggerate their experiences. The written accounts were also limited because in the 14th century few people were literate. Those who wrote about their experiences during the Black Death represented only a narrow portion of society: the wealthy or priests in the Catholic Church. The vast majority of people, particularly those who lived in small towns or the countryside, could leave no account for posterity. Another reason the written accounts are so limited is that in order to write about the Black Death, a person had to survive it. Church and town records, including birth and death rolls, tax rolls, and council minutes, have been used to verify survivors' written accounts. These documents also help historians to understand more about what the plague was like for those who couldn't write about it.

When the scientists decided to analyze the bones of victims to better understand the plague, they already had a healthy respect for the disease. After all, they knew that in the five-year period from 1347 to 1351, the Black Death had killed one-third to one-half of all the people living in Europe.

■   ■   ■

January 1348. London was growing. Nearly 60,000 people lived within its city walls, and thousands of others clustered in nearby villages like Smithfield and Spittle Croft.

At the time, the Catholic Church played a central role in English society, as it did throughout western Europe. Perhaps the adolescent boy whose skeleton was exhumed in Smithfield had left his parents' home for a life of service to the Catholic Church. In the Middle Ages, families often encouraged younger sons to pursue

"MIDDLE AGES": ORIGINS OF A TERM

In the 14th century an Italian poet named Francesco Petrarca, known more widely today as Petrarch, coined the term *Renaissance* to describe the era in which he lived. From the French for "rebirth," the term signified the renewed interest in the classical world of ancient Greece and Rome. After the fall of the Roman Empire in the fifth century, much classical knowledge had been lost. During Petrarch's lifetime, however, Europeans rediscovered the ancient Greek and Roman civilizations through surviving written texts.

People of the Renaissance period also gave a name to the period that preceded their era: they called it the Middle Ages because it came between their time and the ancient world of Greece and Rome. Many felt, wrongly, that the Middle Ages was a period when knowledge completely stagnated. Because of this the Middle Ages has also been called the Dark Ages.

religious careers. Perhaps the boy was even living in the household of the bishop of London, Ralph Stratford.

The family of such a boy would have donated a small portion of land, along with a few sheep and pigs, to the Church as a fee when the boy joined a monastery as an oblate—literally one offered to monastic life. Although sending a son into a religious life meant one less child to care for—a distinct advantage for poor families at the time—a more important reason parents would make such a choice was to show their piety, or devotion to God. In this sense their son was a direct tithe, or offering, to the Church.

If the skeleton exhumed at Smithfield had indeed belonged to a boy who'd entered a monastic order, perhaps the stone carved with a cross, which was found next to his hip, had been a gift to him from his family when he left home. In any event, he may well have kept the stone in a pouch tied around his waist with a string, under the rough brown cloth of his monk's robe, called a habit. Because all traces of fabric disintegrated in the 650 years the boy was buried, however, it's impossible to know for sure.

Medieval Europe was a dirty place. In London most buildings were constructed of wood, with the spaces between timbers filled in with wattle and daub (reeds covered with plaster), which in turn was whitewashed with lime. These wood and plaster buildings afforded a perfect hiding place for rats, fleas, and many other pests.

But it wasn't simply home construction that contributed to unhealthful conditions during the Middle Ages. City streets were narrow. Some could accommodate a cart, but most were wide enough only for a horse or humans. To make matters worse, the streets were unpaved, and the dirt turned to mud every time it rained. The suction of the mud pulling against shoes made walking down the street an adventure. Sidewalks didn't exist, so animals and humans fought for the same space in the streets. Animal droppings accumulated and people threw trash and slop from their windows into the stone or wood-lined open gutter that ran down the center of the street. The king complained that "the streets and lanes through which people had to pass were foul with human faeces and the air of the city poisoned to the great danger of men passing." It took a hard rain to wash the refuse away.

It wasn't that people didn't notice or care. In fact, the problem was so great that the city council of London appointed "scavengers" who had instructions to remove all the filth from the streets and fine those guilty of making the mess. By 1345 there were 40 to 50 men called "rakers" who were equipped with carts to clean up the waste and debris, but the result was anything but sanitary by modern standards.

The biggest problem was the lack of running water. This meant that all household water had to be carried from wells or the River Thames. And since there was no running water, there were no toilets. Only the king and wealthy aristocrats had privies—a primitive form of toilet that was no more than a seat over a hole. These wealthy residents lived in the city, so the waste from the privies was usually piped directly into the River Thames, the same river that provided most of London with water. In 1347 the king complained that his progresses—or trips— down the Thames were being disturbed by the "dung, lay-stalls and other filth" piled up along the bank. Despite their concern, Londoners didn't know how to correct the problem.

The people may have found the mud-filled streets an annoyance on rainy days and noticed the foul smell filling the air on hot days, but they accepted these things as part of

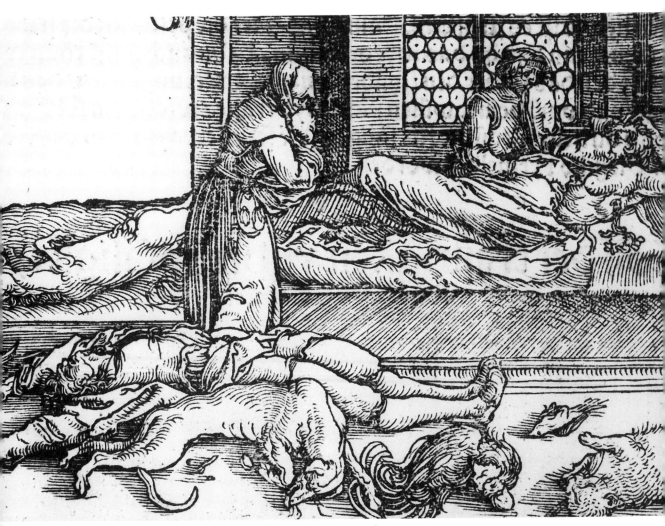

normal city life. They definitely didn't worry that these conditions were a breeding ground for the disease that would come to be known as the Black Death. In 1348 no one had even heard of germs. Most people believed that illness and disease were signs that they had displeased God.

More than a thousand miles southeast of London, on the northwest part of the peninsula that forms modern-day Italy, lay the port of Genoa (in Italian, Genova). In many ways life in this Italian city-state differed little from life in London. Both were great trading centers

This woodcut shows monks praying for a bubonic plague sufferer. Note that the floor is littered with the cadavers of human and animal victims, testimony to the Black Death's destructive power.

regularly visited by ships delivering goods from faraway places. There was one important difference, however. Genoa, located on the Mediterranean Sea in southern Europe, was closer to the great trade routes to the Far East. In the 14th century exotic spices and silks entered the Mediterranean through Constantinople (modern Istanbul, Turkey), where overland caravans arrived from the Far East. After passing Constantinople, goods were brought by sailing ship to important Mediterranean trading centers like Genoa. There they were either moved north across land or, more frequently, transferred to other ships to begin the voyage along the coast of France and Spain. Passing through the narrow Strait of Gibraltar, where the continents of Africa and Europe almost touch, these trade ships would then enter the much colder and rougher Atlantic Ocean. Ships on the Atlantic were bound for northern France, England, or Sweden and the German states. This trading chain from Constantinople to the Mediterranean and through Europe would become the path of the plague.

In Genoa, windy days meant easy sailing for the trade ships—and signaled local men to hurry to the docks in search of work unloading goods. Luck was with the local workers one very windy day in January 1348; three ships were moving rapidly toward land.

As the men worked their way through the noisy streets, dodging the chickens and pigs that were underfoot, rumors were circulating through Genoa. A banking and trade center, Genoa was always a hub of activity. Interesting visitors arrived every day. For more than a year, visitors had been describing a mysterious disease carried by a cloud far, far away to the east. The stories had captured the imagination of some of Genoa's citizens, although most did not take them too seriously. One of the stories described a war between the sea and the sun in the

Indian Ocean. According to the story, the waters of the ocean were pulled up into the sky in a cloud of vapor corrupted by dead and rotting fish. It was said that the sun could not consume the bad vapor, and the vapor could not fall back to earth as rain, so it was drifting around over the ocean, causing illness and suffering.

On the January day when the three ships arrived in port, it seems doubtful that anyone gave a thought to the rumors of illness and suffering to the east. It's more likely that the men hustling to the docks for a chance to unload the ships' cargoes focused only on the possibility that the vessels were carrying valuable goods. Few captains would bring a ship ashore in such strong winds unless they had to. If some of the men did give credence to the rumors of the evil cloud, they probably believed that it was too far away to affect them. In fact, the very ships the men were running to greet would bring terrible suffering and a new kind of fear into their own homes. That evil would come to be known as the Black Death.

CALABRIEN

Regio

SICILIEN

Messina

Origin of a Disease

Berg Monte

Ætna Gibello

View of the Messina harbor. One day in October 1347, a dozen ships arrived in the Italian port with crews stricken by the bubonic plague. Though Messina's citizens forced the ships to sail away, it was too late to save their city from the ravages of the Black Death.

2

No one in Genoa knew that three months before, the plague had landed in the city of Messina, which was located on the island of Sicily, just off the Italian mainland. Like Genoa, Messina was a trading seaport. One day in October 1347, a dozen ships arrived in Messina from the East. Men ran to greet the ships, expecting to find spices and silk. Instead, as the Franciscan friar Michael of Piazza described later, they found "sickness clinging to the very bones" of the sailors. The sailors had been in the town of Messina for only a day or two when its citizens began to fall ill, some dying almost immediately. Panic spread quickly, and the townspeople forced the sailors back onto their ships and made them sail away. Unfortunately, the disease had already infected the citizenry, and hundreds of people began dying every day.

Town officials didn't know what to do. They suggested that those who were still well run to the vineyards and fields of the countryside and save themselves. This spread the disease to the neighboring town of Catania. There, according to Michael of Piazza, "so wicked and timid were the Catanians that they refused to even speak to any from Messina, or to have anything to do with them but quickly fled at their approach."

Such fear was, of course, natural, and fleeing from people sick with the plague actually *did* offer the best chance of staying healthy. But that is not to say that anyone had a rational understanding of the way the plague was transmitted. The disease was assumed to be supernatural in origin and power, and this probably added to the fear surrounding it.

This fear would be incorporated into the stories about the origin of the plague. One story written in Messina said that during a church procession through the streets of the town, citizens saw a black dog carrying a sword in its paws. This dog ran through the procession and entered the church, breaking the lamps and candlesticks on the altar. Historians have theorized that a dog or dogs did appear in the church, possibly knocking items off the altar, or even dragging a sword as if it were a toy. Modern scientists know that dogs did not cause the plague. On the other hand, the dog at the center of the plague story in Messina may have had rabies; rabid animals act strangely. During the plague, however, strange behavior that was normally explicable suddenly became the work of mysterious evil forces.

At the same time that plague was spreading across Sicily, the ships that the townspeople of Messina had driven away landed on the European mainland. It is not known exactly where the ships landed, but soon

after the Sicilian outbreak, in the winter of 1347, the plague appeared along the coast of the Mediterranean Sea in the cities of Tunis, Corsica, Sardinia, and Marseilles. By midsummer the plague had spread into Europe west to the middle of Spain, north through France to the city of Paris, and northeast across all of Italy. Two and a half years later, following the trade routes, the Black Death reached Sweden and Denmark in the north. Even faraway Russia would not be spared as Moscow was struck in 1352. However, before the plague spread, it would devastate Genoa during the winter of 1348.

Survivors in medieval Flanders, in what is now Belgium, are seen burying the dead in coffins. As the plague wore on, such niceties often had to be abandoned, and corpses were simply dumped into open pits. In many towns there weren't even enough able-bodied people to carry away the dead bodies.

The ships that had arrived at Genoa in January 1348 didn't look any different from the others that had arrived in previous years. These ships, called galleys, were commonly used in the Middle Ages for trading and war. They were always in abundance in a powerful and important port such as Genoa. The galleys measured between 100 and 200 feet long and were propelled by sails and oars. Hundreds of sailors—sometimes as many as 1,200—crewed the ships because many men were needed for each heavy oar. The ships might have two or three masts, but all had only one deck, which made them appear to ride low in the water. They were impressive for their beauty and strength.

When the three ships entered port in Genoa, the entire waterfront bustled with activity. After their long sea journey, the sailors eagerly came ashore. Men from Genoa gathered to unload the ships for local merchants. Hours later, the men went home tired and a little richer. While they walked, some might have amused themselves by picking fleas off their sleeves. Fleas were a part of daily life in medieval Europe, and the men were used to the constant itch the bites of the small insects produced. The men had no way of knowing that these fleas were carriers of a deadly disease and that many were about to begin a desperate fight for their lives.

In Genoa, as in other seaports across Europe, travelers had been telling stories of a deadly plague since 1346. The rumors were grim: "India was depopulated, Tartary, Mesopotamia, Syria, Armenia were covered with dead bodies; the Kurds fled in vain to the mountains. In Caramania and Caesara none were left alive," reported one source. Other accounts were more fantastic. "Between Cathay [China] and Persia there rained a vast rain of fire; falling in flakes like snow and burning up mountains and plains and other lands, with men and women; and then arose vast masses of smoke and whosoever beheld this died within the space of half a day; and likewise any man or woman who looked upon those who had seen this."

It is unclear exactly what actual events, if any, these vivid accounts referred to, but they may have been volcanic eruptions or earthquakes. In this prescientific age, people often called upon legend and myth to explain the incomprehensible. Despite these stories, no one thought the mysterious disease would spread to Europe. This is probably because very few Europeans had actually been to the faraway lands of India, Syria, Cathay, and Persia, where many of the goods that arrived in Europe's ports originated. In fact, most Europeans of the Middle Ages never traveled beyond their own city or village. To them news from other areas of Europe would have seemed distant, and news from several thousand miles away might have been a fairy tale.

Rumors *within* a city were taken more seriously. In Genoa alarming news began spreading only days after the arrival of the three ships: sailors had died, and Genoese citizens were sick. Men who had unloaded the ships were some of the first to fall ill. Three days after the ships arrived, many of these men couldn't stand. Their heads hurt and their skin was hot with fever. The next day even dim light hurt their eyes and they were vomiting and giddy. Many were so dazed by the illness that they didn't realize that the other members of their families were also sick.

Although many of the sick lay inside their homes, the sound in the streets outside was nightmarish. Pain and fear had driven victims outside, where their screams and moans filled the air. Others danced wildly through the streets. The houses of wealthy victims were looted, and the poor drank stolen wine to deaden their fear. In the midst of the chaos *becchini*, or corpse carriers, arrived to carry off the dead.

Traditionally, the dead were carried to their graves with great ceremony. Long processions of family, friends, priests, and townspeople would wend their way through the streets, mourning publicly. In the first days of the plague, family members carried bodies of the dead to their funerals, as was the custom. Soon that changed, as there were too few people left to perform the duty, and the able-bodied were too frightened. Some of the desperately poor hired themselves out for the job; these *becchini* were paid either by individuals or by the city. At the height of the plague, once-elaborate funeral processions had shrunk to the *becchini* led by a few priests with candles. The priests would hastily say a prayer as the body was dumped into the nearest open grave. As the plague progressed, the *becchini* sometimes broke into houses, hauling off still-living victims unless the family paid a bribe. In the face of inexplicable disease and increased lawlessness, many citizens who weren't ill fled the city, leaving husbands and wives—even children—to take care of themselves. In some families everyone fell ill, and there was no one left to care for them.

Some local priests tried to fill this need. Despite their education, these men knew no more about the disease than did the most unlearned of victims. With no medicines to give, they comforted their patients in the only way they knew: prayer.

Physicians were even fewer in number than priests. Most neighborhoods had a local priest or vicar (a nonordained clergyman); larger towns with cathedrals or monasteries might have had hundreds of clergy. On the other hand, a medium-sized town might have had one doctor and one surgeon paid by the city to take care of the poor and teach students. There might be another 5 to 10 physicians practicing privately. But no matter how many physicians lived in the town or city, not all citizens had access to them. In general, private physicians attended only the wealthy, whereas the poor had to rely on the care of the city physician. Those who were neither poor nor wealthy might never see a physician. In the raging plague of 1348, it really didn't matter. The physicians didn't know what to do either.

Some families were fortunate in that their neighborhood priest continued to visit, offering what food and drink they could tolerate, departing after saying a hasty prayer. His quick attention might seem uncaring, but it wasn't. To stay in the city and continue to visit the sick, the priest had to be dedicated and brave. He knew that he could only fight the sickness with prayer and, with his fellow priests dying by the hundreds, there was evidence to suggest that this was not enough. In the French town of Perpignan, for example, there were 125 scribes (churchmen who wrote legal documents) before the plague, but only 45 survived. Across Europe priests and monks died in proportion to the people they cared for. In Italy this meant that between 40 percent and 60 percent of the clergy died.

In Genoa the men who unloaded ships had contracted the disease when fleas on the sailors and the merchandise they transported jumped onto them. Some of those fleas had moved into the straw beds the men shared with their families. Some remained on the merchandise and traveled to the homes of the wealthy.

In this way the plague moved rapidly throughout the entire population of Genoa.

Finally, after six days of pain and confusion, some of the early victims (the men who had unloaded the ships) awoke with a clear head. They were thirsty and their bodies ached, but their fever was gone. The next thing many victims noticed was that everyone else in their family was either dead or dying.

The people didn't know anything about the disease except that it killed. They didn't know how to prevent it, how to treat it, or where it came from. They didn't even have a special name for it. The people of Europe simply called the disease a plague or pestilence. Despite the horror that the buboes inspired, the words *plague* and *pestilence* had broad meaning: a disastrous evil or affliction.

Some writers have suggested that the name given to the epidemic, the Black Death, referred to the blackened appearance of the diseased body in the hours before victims died. However, this is incorrect. In fact, the name Black Death was completely unknown to those who experienced the disease. Danish and Swedish chroniclers of the 16th century were the first to give the plague that began in 1348 that name. In the 18th century, four centuries after it had swept through Europe, the term *Black Death* became commonly used. The name, however, was probably the result of a poor translation. When the plague struck in the 14th century, Latin was the language of official and scientific writing across Europe. Two Latin phrases commonly used to describe the plague were *pestis atra* and *atra mors*. Translated into English, *pestis* means "plague" and *mors* means "death." *Atra* could mean "dreadful," "terrible," or "black." Therefore "dreadful death" or "terrible death" could also be translated as "black death." It

is likely that this translation from Latin into another language created the phrase "Black Death," a name that was so descriptive and terrible that it stuck.

Descriptions of the plague by those who saw its victims usually mention the same symptom: the buboes or boils. These growths were vividly described by the Italian author Giovanni Boccaccio, who lived in Florence during the plague. "[I]n men and women alike," Boccaccio wrote, "it first betrayed itself by the emergence of certain tumors in the groin or armpits, some of which grew as large as a common apple, others as an egg, some more, some less, which the common folk called *gavocciolo*."

The bodies of these plague victims show the disease's most recognizable symptom: buboes, boil-like swellings whose appearance usually signaled imminent death.

Other writers described the buboes as knobs, kernels, biles, blaines, blisters, pimples, or wheals; whatever the name, the bulging skin was a distinct and frightening sign of a disease that appeared to have no origin and no cure. Boccaccio wrote about how the *gavocciolo* would spread across the body in all directions. Then "the form of the malady began to change, black spots or livid making their appearance in many cases on the arm or the thigh or elsewhere, now few and large, now minute and numerous. And as the *gavocciolo* had been and still was an infallible token of approaching death, such also were these spots on whomsoever they shewed themselves."

Boccaccio wasn't entirely correct when he asserted that all patients who displayed the buboes died. However, so high was the death toll that he may never have heard of anyone surviving

Guy de Chauliac, physician to the pope's court at Avignon in France, understood that the appearance of buboes did not necessarily mean death. From his observations during the seven months the Black Death ravaged the city of Avignon, he also concluded that there were two different strains, or types, of the disease. (There were actually three, modern scientists believe.) "It has two types," Guy wrote. "The first lasted two months, with continuous fever and spitting of blood, and from this one died in three days. The second lasted for the rest of the period, also with continuous fever but with apostumes and carbuncles on the external parts, principally on the armpits and groin. From this one died in five days."

Based on his observations Guy de Chauliac decided that the first type was more deadly. Other physicians, even if they didn't distinguish between different types, associated spitting blood with certain death: "[M]en

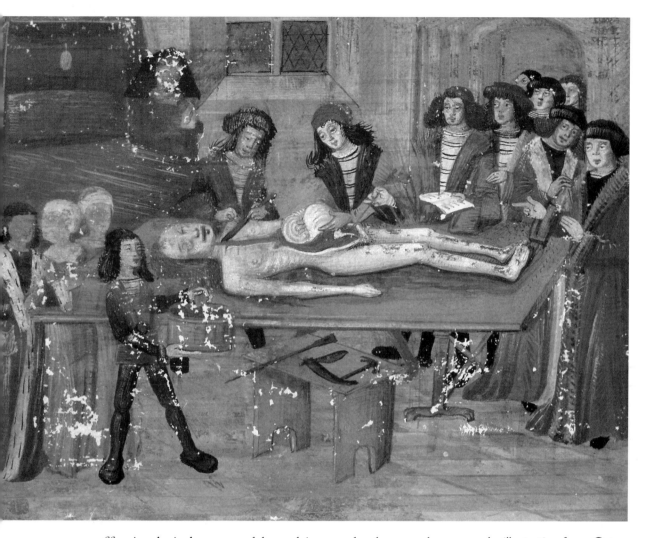

suffer in their lungs and breathing and whoever have these corrupted, or even slightly attacked, cannot by any means escape nor live beyond these two days," one observer wrote. Throughout the course of the disease, there was a great deal of confusion about the length of time a patient could live after falling ill. This confusion was caused by inadequate medical knowledge. It was also caused by the failure to recognize that there were, in fact, three types of plague at work. The failure to recognize the third, and most rapid, form

An illustration from Guy de Chauliac's *Grande Chirugie*, a medical text published in 1363. Guy, physician to the pope, correctly observed that there was more than one strain of the plague.

of the disease only contributed to the general fear that surrounded the sickness.

Guy de Chauliac made reference to victims who died two or five days after the worst of the buboes formed; other medieval chroniclers noted even swifter death. Geoffrey the Baker wrote of villagers going peacefully to bed, apparently in full health, then not awaking the next morning, having been struck by the plague in the night. Simon of Covino described priests and doctors who were "seized by the plague whilst administering spiritual aid; and, often by a single touch, or a single breath of the plague-stricken, perished even before the sick person they had come to assist." Modern medicine tells us that death could not result instantly from contact with plague victims. Those who apparently did die instantly had probably contracted a rapidly acting form of the disease and were near death before they even noticed the symptoms. In a time of panic, the onset of fast-acting symptoms might pass unnoticed, making it appear that the victim had contracted the disease and died immediately.

Medical knowledge during this period did not include an understanding of the ways a disease might be transmitted. Because of this, even educated men talked of the poisonous cloud that was said to spread the plague. This did not mean that transmission of the disease was absent from medical discussions. In general, one group of educated men believed in the existence of the poisonous cloud, and the other believed in person-to-person transmission. Adding to the puzzle was the speed with which the disease traveled, appearing one day in a new region and mysteriously vanishing from another, not halted by cold or change of season. The speed with which the plague conquered

Europe was so great that even today it is regarded as a marvel. In an era when people traveled by foot, horseback, or wagon, and therefore fairly slowly, the plague crossed Europe faster than cholera did in the 1800s, when train and steamship travel was common.

The Year 1348

3

In 1348 an important diplomatic, religious, and political event was planned: the marriage of 15-year-old Princess Joan of England to Prince Pedro of Castile. Elaborate plans had been made for this match, which would link two ruling dynasties. Ships had been commissioned to transport the princess and her entourage from England to the Spanish kingdom of Castile. In addition to Joan's many ladies-in-waiting and serving people, the group included 100 bowmen along with important diplomats and clergymen. Prince Pedro had even sent a court minstrel for his betrothed's entertainment. An entire ship was needed to carry Joan's belongings and clothing. As evidence of her piety, the princess traveled with a portable private chapel outfitted with silver altar vessels, each worth more than a million dollars in modern currency.

After crossing the English Channel, the princess and her traveling party would stop in France to collect provisions for the journey to Castile. When they arrived in Bordeaux in August 1348, the mayor greeted them with the news that plague had struck his city. That fact could hardly have escaped the visitors, as hundreds of bodies were stacked in the streets and on the docks. The stench of the decaying bodies was overwhelming, but the princess and her entourage, used to smelly streets, simply covered their noses with perfumed handkerchiefs and proceeded to the royal chateau.

EQUAL OPPORTUNITY KILLER

When the plague arrived, European society was divided along rigid lines, with everyone belonging to one of four groups: Church, nobility, urban dwellers, or peasants. People clearly understood their social position and for the most part couldn't change it.

Priests, monks, nuns, and higher officials such as bishops formed the first social group—representatives of the Catholic Church, which at the time was the only Christian church. In an age when few people could read and write, the clergy were literate, and frequently they assisted kings and lords in governing. The medieval Church had vast landholdings and enjoyed enormous wealth, but its greatest power came from the spiritual authority it exercised. Religion played a major role in the lives of most people of the time, and the vast majority of Europeans were Catholic.

The second group in the medieval hierarchy was the nobility. In some regions the nobility made their homes in towns; other nobles lived in fortified castles. Whatever the case, the nobles' wealth and status was linked to their inherited control of large amounts of land, villages, and peasant labor. Nobles did not work the fields themselves, but instead relied on the peasants to raise the crops and animals that fed and clothed Europe. The nobles received a portion of the peasants' production in the form of a tax. The nobility traveled frequently, supervising the different areas of land they owned and collecting taxes. In general nobles preferred to live near the land that formed the basis of their wealth and power.

Though ideally situated for defense against an invading enemy, the chateau was, unfortunately for the princess, near the port, whose docks swarmed with rats infested by plague-carrying fleas. Within days the young princess saw her companions fall ill. Understanding little about the spread of the disease, the remaining members of the group did not flee. Because of this the chateau quickly became a death trap. The princess's chancellor died first. Twelve days later, on September 2, Princess Joan succumbed to the Black Death.

The entire area surrounding the port was so badly

The third group, the urban dwellers, consisted of a broad range of people, from wealthy merchants to craftsmen to beggars. A strong merchant class meant that a town had goods to sell, which in turn meant that other wealthy members of society would visit the town to make purchases. Important markets would develop and cathedrals would be built, all of which benefited the members of the community. The growing towns of Europe were also home to craftsmen and unskilled workers. The craftsmen produced tanned animal hides for clothing or writing parchment, made furniture, built houses and city walls, and, in general, performed the skilled work associated with daily life. Below this group were the unskilled workers and urban poor. They struggled to survive, often living out-of-doors and eating leftover scraps.

The last group of people living in medieval Europe had little contact with the cities. They were the peasants, or serfs. By law the men, women, and children of the peasantry were tied to the land they worked. This meant that a peasant family lived in the same place generation after generation regardless of the changing prosperity of the surrounding village. The peasants owed a portion of their labor, to be paid in the form of goods, to the owner of their land, which was either the local lord or the Church. They had no voice in the making of laws.

The Europeans may have understood and accepted this rigid social structure, but the plague did not. It struck all classes with equal ferocity, snuffing out the lives of princesses and beggars alike.

affected by plague that the mayor of Bordeaux decided to set it on fire, hoping to halt the advance of the disease. The fire grew out of control and spread from the docks to the city and chateau. Meanwhile, Princess Joan's father, Edward III of England, learned of her death and paid the bishop of Carlisle the equivalent of $2,000 a day in modern currency to go to Bordeaux and retrieve her body. Despite this incentive, the bishop was unsuccessful. It's possible that he was truly unable to find her body because it had been consumed in the fire. More likely, however, the bishop was so frightened by the prospect of visiting the plague-ridden city that he didn't actually travel to Bordeaux.

Edward III wrote a letter to Prince Pedro's father soon after the princess's death. In it he called her a martyred angel sent to heaven so she could intercede with God on behalf of her family. Although Joan's death was a heavy diplomatic and personal blow, Edward III, in typical medieval fashion, was most concerned that his family had displeased God and was being punished. Despite his wealth and power, Edward could neither prevent his daughter's death nor fully understand why it had happened.

It was only at the beginning of the 20th century, more than 500 years after it disappeared, that the origin of the Black Death was finally established. The original form of the Black Death was the bubonic plague, which was—and still is—endemic, or permanently resident, in certain areas of the world. At the time of the Black Death, regions where the bubonic plague was endemic were sparsely populated. Periodically the disease would infect local people, killing a high proportion, then spread slowly with travelers or along trade routes. As the disease gradually spread outward from the endemic region, an occasional epidemic—a period when large numbers of people in a certain area were infected simultaneously—would occur. Several hundred years after the initial outbreak, the plague would disappear, retreating to the regions where it was endemic. In this cycle of active epidemic periods and nearly dormant endemic periods, there have been three recorded pandemics of the plague—that is, three instances when the disease occurred over a wide region and affected a very large number of people.

The first recorded outbreak of plague, which occurred among the Philistines in 1320 B.C., is described in the Bible. However, this was only an isolated outbreak. The first pandemic started in Arabia and moved to Egypt in A.D. 542. Over the next 100 years it moved through the Mediterranean region, sweeping across the remains of the Roman Empire, then traveling north across Europe to England. This plague ended its journey sometime after 664, having lasted 122 years and claimed the lives of an estimated 100 million people.

The second pandemic was the plague eventually called the Black Death. It reached the Far East in 1347, surged across Europe until 1350, and died out in 1351. This was only the end of the initial outbreak, however. The plague would continue to emerge and claim victims for three centuries until its grand finale, the Great Plague of London. That occurred in 1665— 319 years after the plague first emerged from its endemic state.

The third, and last, pandemic started in 1892 in China and reached Bombay, India, in 1896. Millions died in this last pandemic—6 million in India alone. Europe was largely spared, although plague appeared

This 13th-century French manuscript illustrates the first recorded outbreak of plague, which occurred among the Philistines in 1320 B.C. and which is described in the Bible. As was characteristic of artwork during the Middle Ages, the ancients are depicted in medieval surroundings and wearing medieval clothes.

briefly in Suffolk, England, in 1910. There, fortunately, only a few people died. Technically this last pandemic has not ended because plague still appears occasionally. Records kept by the World Health Organization show that between the years 1954 and 1997 plague was reported in 38 countries. Seven countries, including the United States, have had at least one outbreak almost every year.

Dr. Robert Pollitzer, an expert on the Black Death, has concluded that the medieval plague originated in central Asia. Pollitzer based his beliefs on the findings of a Russian archaeologist who discovered records of unusually high death rates in 1338 and 1339 in that region. Because this area is still one in which plague is endemic, Pollitzer has concluded that the Black Death emerged there, then spread eastward into China, south to India, and west to Europe.

Even if medieval people had associated the plague with fleas, they would have been unable to understand how the flea carried the disease without dying. This is because medieval people did not have knowledge of the microorganisms that caused plague.

The plague begins with a specific bacillus, or rod-shaped bacterium, named *Yersinia pestis. Y. pestis* lives in the bloodstream of a mammal or the stomach of a flea. These hosts carry the disease but are not made sick.

Most fleas live in hair or fur. A popular, though incorrect, belief is that the fleas carrying the Black Death got their start on the backs of rats. In fact, the plague-carrying fleas first lived in the thick fur of the *tarbagan,* or Manchurian marmot. This squirrel-like animal was hunted for its skin. Other small rodents, such as the jerboa and the suslik, also played an early role as carriers of the host flea.

If the plague bacillus continues to live in its host flea, it is not a threat. In order for the disease to spread, the rodent carrying the host flea has to leave its home and take the host flea with it to a place where it can migrate to humans or other animals that are susceptible to the disease. Flood and drought probably caused the rodents' migration, which in turn started the Black Death. This idea matches the accounts of disasters coming from the East beginning in the early 14th century. With their food supply diminished by the unusual weather, rodents such as the marmot, jerboa, and suslik moved out of their usual habitat in search of nourishment. That brought these squirrel-like animals into contact with another rodent—the famous black rat, hardy and a natural vagabond. The rat, in turn, often lived around humans, and fleas that it had picked up from the other rodents sometimes transferred to people. Thus, many scientists believe, the initial movement of the plague bacillus away from its natural hosts and into human society can be traced largely to the black rat and other rodents.

Not everyone shares that belief, however. In the opinion of a historian named B. Jorge, the role of the rat in the spread of the plague has been overrated. He cites as evidence the fact that little mention is made of increased numbers of rats in medieval accounts of the plague. Professor Jorge believes that a flea not living on a plague-carrying rat could transmit the disease directly from person to person. How? By biting an infected human, then transferring some of the bacillus-filled blood to the next person it bit. The general hypothesis that rats weren't necessarily essential in the transmission of the Black Death has found support from, among other authorities, the 1910 Plague Research Committee, which reported that

"the transference of infected rats and fleas in merchandise or, in the case of fleas, on the body of a human being, must be considered." It has been proven that a carrier flea can live without a host animal for up to a month. The flea could travel alone for hundreds of miles, for example, while living in cargo on a ship. There is one documented case of a flea living for six months in a rat burrow without the nourishment of

This scanning electron micrograph shows a flea clinging to the fur of a rat. Especially prevalent in the unhygienic cities of the Middle Ages, fleas carried the bacteria that caused the plague.

a host animal. This means that fleas without host rats could have transmitted the disease.

All three plague pandemics have probably been a combination of three types of plague: bubonic, septicemic, and pneumonic. The bubonic was the initial and most famous form taken by the medieval Black Death. The second form, septicemic (meaning that it affected the blood), was the fastest acting. The pneumonic, or pulmonary, strain (affecting the lungs) was the deadliest. Each strain had a different way of attacking a victim's body.

The bubonic strain was readily identified by the buboes that appeared on the victims' bodies. These swellings of a lymph gland usually appeared in the groin (the word *bubo* comes from the Greek word for "groin"), but they often occurred in the armpit or on the neck as well. The swelling was caused by the lymph gland's absorption of infective material. Although death usually came within five days, some patients did survive an attack of the bubonic plague.

The septicemic form worked much faster. Like the bubonic plague, it was carried by infected fleas, but the infectious microorganisms moved immediately into the bloodstream, causing chills, fever, and—if the patient lived long enough—secondary abscesses, including buboes. Usually, however, a victim of septicemic plague was dead long before the buboes had time to develop. This was the form that some chroniclers were referring to when they wrote about apparently healthy people who would sicken overnight and be dead by dawn.

Other stories of rapid death were also recorded. In Spain, a traveler spent the night at an inn taking "dinner with his host (and his host's daughters and servant, all of whom appeared to be in good health)."

The traveler paid for his night's lodging in advance and went to bed. The next morning the traveler realized he needed to see the innkeeper but could not find him. Finally, with the help of others, he discovered that the innkeeper, his daughters, and the servant had all died during the night. Understandably, the traveler left in great haste. These victims almost certainly had the septicemic form of plague.

The plague-carrying flea may have been the single greatest contributor to the spread of the septicemic form. After feeding off a bloodstream full of plague bacilli, it could carry enough of the infection to its next human host. A modern scientist would refer to this invasion of the bloodstream as septicemia; a layperson might call it blood poisoning. This was the fastest acting of the three forms of plague that struck medieval Europe.

The third form, the pneumonic plague, was carried by neither rat nor flea. Instead, the bacilli, which were concentrated in the victim's lungs, adhered to microscopic droplets of blood and sputum that the victim expelled by coughing or even by simply breathing. Lingering in the air, these contaminated droplets could infect anyone who moved through their path.

In the late 19th century, when the various strains of plague were identified, treatment still had not advanced much beyond that of the medieval period. However, 19th-century physicians were able to figure out how deadly each strain was. When a mild epidemic struck in the 1800s, those infected by the bubonic plague had a 60 percent to 90 percent chance of dying. A similar mortality rate probably prevailed during the medieval plague. In both periods an even smaller proportion of those stricken by the pneumonic strain survived. The difference was that in the 19th century physicians could tell the difference between the three strains. In the medieval period the rapid death of some patients was simply a mystery. Bubonic plague in the 19th century would kill within four to seven days. In the Manchurian epidemic of 1921, in which the pneumonic strain struck, life expectancy was a mere 44 hours.

Not only was the pneumonic strain more lethal, it was also more contagious than the other two strains. Although those who lived through the medieval plague would not have believed it, the bubonic plague is actually not particularly contagious. The lungs aren't affected, and the patient usually dies or has recovered before enough bacilli are in the bloodstream to permit flea-borne transmission to another person. Because it attacked the lungs and triggered coughing—thus unleashing aerosolized bacilli—the pneumonic strain was much more contagious.

It was probably the combination of the three strains that made the Black Death spread so quickly and with such disastrous results. It was also this combination that allowed the disease to travel in unexpected directions by leaps and bounds. The septicemic strain added to the speed with which the disease could kill and made it easier for humans to contract the illness through fleabites. And while a hard frost would normally kill off the carrier fleas and halt the spread of disease, because the pneumonic strain could be transmitted from human to human without a carrier flea, the plague raged on even with the arrival of winter.

Taken together, the three strains of the plague that struck Europe in 1348 earned their name Black Death. In the path of an unseen, incurable, and fast-moving disease, the people of Europe faced a world that looked darker and more forbidding than anything they had previously imagined. Perhaps an Italian plague survivor named Agniolo di Tura said it best: "and nobody wept no matter what his loss, because almost everyone expected death. . . . And people said and believed, 'This is the end of the world.'"

And It Rained Snakes

"There was a rain of frogs, serpents, lizards, scorpions, and many venomous beasts of that sort," wrote a 14th-century traveler to India. Such reports, which circulated widely in Europe, undoubtedly contained fanciful elements. But beginning in 1333 a series of natural disasters did strike the Far East, and these disasters played a role in unleashing the Black Death.

4

Life in 14th-century Europe was very similar from town to town and city to city. The 11th and 12th centuries had been quite prosperous. The Crusades—expeditions undertaken by Christian knights to win back the Holy Land from the Muslims—had provided activity for the many people who chose to participate. Those who stayed home expanded the fields, plowing under forests to grow more food for the burgeoning population. Even the climate had been kind. Warm weather had allowed better harvests and helped people live longer and easier lives. And the land was worth more. From the year 1000 to the year 1300, the value of land in Europe had increased 17 times, while the rents paid to farm the land remained nearly the same. Because of this the serfs—peasants who were legally obligated to live on the land they worked—

were better off than before. But by the 14th century, the great economic growth had ended.

Changes had begun around the year 1300, as the population of the countryside began to catch up with the amount of food peasants were able to produce. Cities were becoming overcrowded, which meant that more people were competing for the same jobs. In the Italian province of Tuscany, the population had reached an estimated 1.18 million before the coming of the plague. After the plague, Tuscany's population would not reach this level again until the middle of the 19th century, 500 years later.

Beginning in 1333—more than 10 years before the plague ravaged Europe—a series of natural disasters struck the Far East. In China, the year 1333 started with drought and famine. Flooding of the rivers Kiang and Hoai, which took a toll of more than 400,000 lives, soon followed. But the string of disasters didn't stop. According to witnesses, the mountain Tsinsheou "fell in," which probably referred to an earthquake.

The year 1334 was no better. In the Houkouang and Honan regions of China the year began with drought, then swarms of locusts arrived. In the mountains of Ki-Ming-Chan, an earthquake caused a lake several hundred miles in circumference to form. From 1337 to 1345, earthquakes and floods periodically struck, and locusts continued to swarm. Accounts of these calamities reached Europe just as tales of the problems a bit closer, in India, circulated.

A cleric from northern Europe who was traveling through India wrote back about what he saw:

In the East, hard by Greater India, in a certain province, horrors and unheard of tempests overwhelmed the whole province for the space of three

days. On the first day there was a rain of frogs, serpents, lizards, scorpions, and many venomous beasts of that sort. On the second, thunder was heard, and lightening and sheets of fire fell upon the earth, mingled with hail stones of marvelous size; which slew almost all, from the greatest even to the least. On the third day there fell fire from heaven and stinking smoke, which slew all that were left of men and beasts, and burned up all the cities and towns in those parts. By these tempests the whole province was infected; and it is conjectured that, through the foul blast of wind that came from the South, the whole seashore and surrounding lands were infected, and are waxing more and more poisonous from day to day.

Lacking a rational, scientific explanation for the plague, many people during the Middle Ages—even among the educated—attributed the Black Death to supernatural causes such as a cloud of bad air sent by God to punish sinful humankind.

This account, and others like it, formed the basis of the mythical evil cloud that was talked about in Europe. Although these stories of death and destruction were greatly exaggerated, the plague did have devastating effects. Between 1347 and 1351, approximately 30 million Europeans—an estimated one-third to one-half of the entire population of the continent—would die of plague. In Africa and Asia another 20 million people would perish.

Life had always been precarious in medieval Europe. In almost every family some children died before reaching adulthood. Many women died in childbirth. The experience of Valorino de Barna Ciuriani was typical. In his memoirs he wrote about the death of his father, five daughters, three sons, and wife, plus numerous newborn children. The rituals associated with losing a family member were close, personal, and familiar. Despite this familiarity, the plague brought a new level of horror to facing death. In most places plague remained in the village or city for several months. During this period one of every two or three people died. Parents went to bed at night wondering if their children would be alive in the morning. One child might die one day and another three months later. Adding to the mental anguish was the lack of pattern. Sometimes entire families perished; other times, for no apparent reason, one parent would die and the other live, or several children would die while their siblings—who lived under the same roof and shared the same bed—survived. An entire family might be killed while another living nearby was completely spared. One village might be destroyed while another was passed over. The pious died at the same rate as the wicked. Why was this? Most of the people who lived through the plague attributed it to the will of God.

The perceived relationship between God and plague resulted in several attitudes toward religion in general and the Catholic Church in particular: anger, renewed piety, and the development of fanatical sects. Many who felt anger toward the Church believed that its priests and bishops should have foreseen and stopped the "bad behavior" that caused God's wrath. In short, the Church should have warned people that they were behaving improperly.

This anger only increased when people saw or heard about priests abandoning sick people. One monk in England wrote, "In this plague many chaplains and hired parish priests would not serve without excessive pay." Another chronicler complained that "parishes remained altogether unserved and beneficed parsons have turned away from the care of the benefices for fear of death." These benefices were the churches, towns, and people the priest was to serve in exchange for money and privilege from the local lord. The common view seems to have been that the priests left their benefices to save themselves. However, this is probably an unfair assessment. There were a few notorious examples of priests fleeing their religious flocks. However, church records show that priests in villages died in great numbers; in fact, roughly half of the clergy in England died during the plague. Since these men were more likely to have the financial resources to allow them to flee, the great numbers who died indicate that most remained with their flock.

Despite this, the Church and the wealth that it represented were a target for anger. In December 1349, the English bishop of Bath and Wells, John of Shrewsbury, left his home after the plague had subsided and attended a special service of thanksgiving at the town of Yeovil. During the service, the church was attacked by what the bishop called "sons of perdition (hell)" armed with bows, arrows, iron bars, and other weapons. The "siege" on the church lasted two days. The assailants were members of the community living in a state of shock and horror at the number of dead in their village. If God had been responsible for the plague, then perhaps the best way to react was to let his representatives on earth know how angry and confused they felt.

In spite of the perception that individual priests were leaving their posts, people remained firm believers in both God and the Catholic Church. The number of wills hastily written at home rose immensely during the plague, causing one man to remark that people loved their lawyers as much as their priests. However, these hastily drawn-up wills were often the result of a desire to atone for sins, which popular belief held had caused the plague. Many men promised to donate their entire estate to the Church if they died. Motivations for this included a true belief in the necessity of atoning for sins, the desire to placate God and perhaps save other family members, and terror. Many children lost their parents to plague only to discover that their father's last will, written on his deathbed, had given their inheritance to the Catholic Church. Inheritance was central to a family's survival, and these children had to find work, and sometimes a place to live, quickly and with few resources.

The third reaction to the Church during the plague was a more extreme form of devotion. The "Brotherhood of the Flagellants," also called the "Brethren of the Cross," was a movement that originated in eastern Europe among monks. These monks, and the people who joined them, firmly believed that

(continued on page 57)

WHIPPING AWAY SIN: THE BROTHERHOOD OF THE FLAGELLANTS

The Brotherhood of the Flagellants, a group that sought to atone for the sins its members believed had caused God to unleash the plague, maintained a high degree of discipline. Newcomers, who had to have the permission of their wives to join, also had to make a full confession of their sins. As an initiation they promised to scourge, or whip, themselves three times a day for 33 days and 8 hours—I day for each year of Christ's life. In addition, they had to prove that they had enough money to pay the daily fee for food while on pilgrimage through the countryside. Absolute obedience to the group master was demanded, and all members promised not to shave, bathe, sleep in a bed, change clothes, or talk to a member of the opposite sex.

The Flagellant movement was strongest in the northern countries in Europe. The arrival of the Flagellants provided excitement and emotional release for residents of small, isolated villages; but more important, it signaled the possibility of preventing or shortening the duration of plague. Most villagers had little to lose by attending the spectacles.

The Flagellants marched into towns solemnly and in two files. Led by the group master and two lieutenants, they were an impressive sight, with their heads and faces hidden by hoods called cowls, and their eyes fixed firmly on the ground. Dressed in somber clothes with red crosses on back, front, and hood, they remained silent except for the occasional singing of hymns. Their arrival in a town would be heralded by the ringing of church bells, after which townsfolk would greet them and lead them to the church. A few parish priests tried to prevent the Flagellants from using the local church—the official Catholic hierarchy took a dim view of the Brother-hood's activities—but such efforts seem to have served only to anger the townspeople, who generally wanted to see the spectacle. Smart parish priests stayed out of the way.

Though the initial part of the Flagellants' ceremony took place in the church, they preferred to conduct their services in the open air, usually in a marketplace. There they would form a circle and strip to the waist, retaining only a linen cloth or skirt that stretched to their ankles. They would pile their discarded clothing inside the circle. Often the sick of the village would enter to touch the clothing for its supposed healing power. On at least one occasion desperate parents laid a dead child in the circle in hope of a miracle.

While the townspeople looked on, the Flagellants would march around in a circle until the master gave the order to drop to the ground. They would fall in postures reflecting their sins (for example, a liar would fall on his side and hold up three fingers) or in imitation of the crucifixion. The master would beat some of the members individually, then signal the collective flagellation.

For this each member carried a heavy scourge made up of three or four leather thongs, each tipped with metal studs. Each member would rhythmically beat his back and breast, with three of the Brethren leading the ceremony with the master, encouraging the members to pray for mercy on all sinners. During the flagellation, townspeople groaned and sobbed in encouragement, urging the Brethren to greater excess.

At the height of the movement, the Flagellants traveled in the thousands. One monastery in Holland had to help house and feed 2,500 of the Flagellant pilgrims within a period of six months. In two and a half months 5,300 Flagellants visited the monastery of Tournai. Initially the Catholic Church did not officially support or oppose the movement. In May 1348 Pope Clement VI attended ceremonies of public flagellation at Avignon. However, Clement quickly realized that he could not control the Flagellants or the crowds who came to see them. On October 20, 1349, the church officially denounced the Flagellants for their contempt of church discipline and performance of acts contrary to accepted observances.

(continued from page 54)

the sins of the people had caused God to send the plague. In particular, many Brethren conceived of the Black Death as retribution for the "avarice, greed and usurious oppression of the poor." Some blamed the behavior of certain women. The chronicler Knighton, for example, wrote about "the indignation of the people because, when tournaments were held, in almost every place, a band of women would arrive as if they had come to join the sport, dressed in a variety of the most sumptuous male costumes. . . . They were even known to wear those knives which are called 'daggers'. . . ; and thus they spent or rather squandered their possessions, and wearied their bodies with fooleries

This illustration, from a medieval hymnal, depicts the Brotherhood of the Flagellants. In the midst of the plague, the wandering monks whipped themselves to show their piety.

and wanton buffoonery." Knighton pointed out that "God, in his manner, brought marvelous remedy." But the chronicler didn't feel the need to counter the sins he observed the way some people did.

Those who joined the Brethren of the Cross adopted flagellation—self-administered whippings —as a method of proving their piety, or loyalty, to God. The Flagellants would move through the countryside, marching two-by-two in a column 200 to 1,000 strong. Although chroniclers record numerous daily performances of public flagellation with massive amounts of blood flowing, this must have been an exaggeration. The rules of the Brethren did not allow bathing or changing clothes, and without disinfectants the monks would have quickly been made ill by their activities. Historians have suggested two alternative explanations: that the most violent performances were reserved for important towns or that a few of the Brethren were singled out to perform at each ceremony, allowing them time to recover afterward.

Their collective hysteria, which was translated into their public performances, may have been, under other circumstances, disgusting to some people. However, many people living in constant fear of plague found comfort in the Flagellants' visits. Most townspeople felt that they were protected from the plague just by watching the performances of the Brethren. The Flagellant movement lost its place at center stage when the plague years were over.

Unfortunately for all who lived through the plague, none of their actions and involvement with the Church helped prevent the spread of the disease. Although many people died at peace because they had given their belongings to the Church, had been comforted on their deathbed by a priest, or had witnessed a great Flagellant spectacle, these things were only helpful emotionally. Real medical help was left to physicians and surgeons.

Following in the long tradition of Hippocrates and Galen, physicians were regarded as educated men, even if their training during the Middle Ages dealt more with philosophy than anatomy. Physicians of the time still adhered to the Hippocratic and Galenic methods

INFLUENCES ON MEDIEVAL MEDICINE

The traditions inherited from Hippocrates of Cos (ca. 460–ca. 377 B.C.) and Galen of Pergamum (A.D. 129–ca. 199) dominated medicine throughout the medieval period. Hippocrates and his followers are famous for their efforts to establish standards for medicine at a time when physicians didn't study in formal schools. Today, medical school graduates take the Hippocratic oath, which embodies a code of medical ethics pioneered by Hippocrates. In addition to their emphasis on the proper behavior of doctors, the Hippocratics were among the first to say that the gods did not directly cause sickness or disease. They offered instructions for examination procedures, diagnosis, and prognosis (prediction of the course a disease will take). The physician was "to examine the patient's face, hands, eyes, posture, breathing, sleep, stool, urine, vomit, and sputum." The physician "was also to notice coughing, sneezing, hiccuping, flatulence, fever, convulsions, pustules, tumors, and lesions."

Five hundred years after Hippocrates, Galen of Pergamum believed, as had his predecessor, that the human body was composed of blood, phlegm, yellow bile, and black bile (known as the four humors), which in turn were associated with the basic qualities hot, cold, wet, and dry. For his diagnosis Galen relied on the pulse and examination of urine. However, he was also interested in understanding the internal workings of the body. Dissection was against the law in Greece, so Galen recommended that physicians travel to Alexandria in Egypt, where they could examine a human cadaver. The writings of Galen, together with the Hippocratics, encouraged a rational approach that dominated the practice of medicine for more than a thousand years into and beyond the medieval period.

Hippocrates and Galen. The two ancient physicians deeply influenced doctors of the Middle Ages.

of examining the body—they observed the fluids and temperature. They were concerned with predicting the course of a disease, not preventing it. Surgeons and barbers were less respected. They were left with the more physical labor of setting broken bones, mending wounds, and pulling teeth.

Physicians would have been familiar with what Galen said, in the second century A.D., about the spread of disease: he blamed the inhalation of infected air (an idea that, with the pneumonic form of the plague at least, wasn't too far off). Galen wrote that the "beginning of the putrescence [or decaying smell] may be a multitude of unburned corpses, as may happen in war; or the exhalations of marshes and ponds in summer." Following this relatively straightforward (and rational) idea of infection, many physicians of the 14th century propounded bad-air theories to explain the plague.

Ibn Khâtimah, a prominent Arab philosopher and physician from Granada, postulated that the air that brought plague had been permanently transformed by corruption. At the heart of this cloud of bad air, he believed, no light would burn and no man could live. On the edge of this cloud was an area of partial corruption where death was not inevitable. Ibn Khâtimah thought that the bad air had been caused by recent weather.

Others did not agree that the air was permanently transformed. Ibn al Khatîb, a colleague and friend of Ibn Khâtimah, believed that the air was only temporarily altered. Alfonso of Córdoba carried that idea further. He believed that the movements of the planets had probably started the problem, but added that the poisoning of the atmosphere was the result of human action. He continued by explaining how this could be done. Air could be infected artificially by a preparation in a glass flask. Then the "person who wishes to do that evil waits till there is a strong, slow wind from some region of the world, then goes into the wind and rests his flask against some rocks opposite the city or town which he wishes to infect and, making a wide detour and going further into the wind lest the vapors infect him, pulls his flask violently against the rocks. When it breaks the vapour pours out and is dispersed in the air, and whoever it touches will die."

Aside from herbal medicines used in the treatment of minor ailments, medieval physicians had few effective ways to combat disease. One of the most common treatments for all kinds of conditions, adjustment of the "humors" through bloodletting (shown at the left of this woodcut), was totally useless against the plague.

These farfetched explanations gave doctors no direction for countering the plague. In fact, physicians had few effective weapons against the spread of plague and no medicines to treat it. Their first thought was to close up the houses of plague victims, fastening shutters or tapestries over the windows to prevent the disease from moving in and out with the air. Bathing was also regarded as dangerous because it opened the pores to the airborne disease. The plague was in fact a contributing factor in the decline in bathing over the next few centuries in Europe. In place of bathing, the wealthy routinely rubbed their skin with cologne to conceal the smell of their unwashed bodies. The less affluent might wash their faces and hands in vinegar.

Another common bit of advice was to do nothing. Physicians recommended complete inactivity as a method to avoid contact with the plague. If people had to move, then they were advised to do so slowly. Exercise, it was believed, introduced more air into the body and therefore more poison.

This does not mean that medieval physicians were without any methods of treatment for other illnesses. They had valuable knowledge of healing herbs for headache and minor stomachache. Treatment for more serious ailments relied on the adjustment of the "humors" (body fluids) by bloodletting. And surgeons had the ability to amputate limbs and cauterize bleeding wounds. Unfortunately, none of this was helpful in combating the plague.

Physicians also still used astrology, believing that the position of celestial objects influenced human affairs. The king of France, Philip VI, ordered a report on the origin of the plague from the medical faculty of the University of Paris. The report stated that on March 20, 1345, at 1 P.M. there had been a conjunction of Saturn, Jupiter, and Mars in the house of Aquarius. The conjunction of Saturn and Jupiter was notorious for death and disaster, and the conjunction of Mars and Jupiter spread pestilence. As Philip could see, the conjunction of all three planets spelled disaster. This was the most prestigious report on the origin of the plague issued at the time, but it was not the best informed.

Some physicians were more experimental in their treatments, incorporating gold and crushed pearls into tonics. Another treatment called for a powder of sulfur, arsenic, and antimony to be thrown on the fire in a victim's home. Today we know that sulfur is destructive to fleas, bacteria, and rats (the other parts of the powder probably helped cover bad smells in the house), so this remedy probably did some good and little harm. Pills of aloe, myrrh, and saffron were also popular.

Gentile of Foligno, an eminent physician in the Italian cities of Bologna and Perugia, suggested powdered emerald as a cure. Treacle, or *theriac,* was the most prized and expensive of medicines in medieval Europe. The recipes for its use were varied; however, it was almost always composed of snake's flesh. A 15th-century English book of medical advice suggested that treacle be given twice a day during plague; the compound should be dissolved in clear wine, clear ale, or rosewater and taken well before meals. During the initial outbreak of the Black Death, Gentile of Foligno was the period's greatest advocate of the use of treacle. He maintained that the treacle must be at least a year old and that children should not ingest it but have it rubbed on them. Gentile himself died of the Black Death.

The use of snake in treacle was important. Snakes, which figure prominently in several Bible stories, represented both good and evil to medieval people. In addition, stories had circulated that in the Far East it had rained serpents in the years before the plague struck Europe. Some suggested that during earthquakes in China reptiles had been released from the ground along with the corrupt air that caused the disease. One of the Black Death's victims, Henry of Grosmont, duke of Lancaster, wrote in his book on medicine that "treacle is made of poison so it can destroy other poisons." Although Henry was more interested in the spiritual reasoning behind the use of treacle, his general idea was correct. Small amounts of a poisonous substance can be ingested to build up resistance to larger amounts. The introduction of a nonlethal disease triggers the body's production of antibodies. Antibodies will protect the body from infection by a related, potentially lethal disease. This

An illuminated manuscript from the Middle Ages depicts treatments for various illnesses. For plague victims, doctors prescribed tonics of gold and crushed pearls, bloodletting, treacle (a medicine composed of snake flesh), powdered emeralds, and pills made of aloe, saffron, and myrrh. These remedies probably did little harm but were ineffective against the Black Death.

is how modern vaccinations work. Unfortunately for Henry of Grosmont, neither snakes nor treacle had anything to do with the Black Death.

Despite their lack of resources, many physicians conducted themselves admirably in the face of the plague. This is not to suggest that there are records of physicians miraculously saving great numbers of patients. Based on the knowledge and resources available at the time, modern science tells us, that would have been impossible. Instead, physicians won fame because of their courage and decision to remain with their patients. Records indicate that many doctors died or fled within the first weeks of plague. The pope's physician Guy de Chauliac, who was one of the profession's most distinguished members, said: "The plague was shameful for physicians, who could give no help at all, especially as out of fear of infection, they hesitated to visit the sick. Even if they did they achieved nothing, and earned no fees, for all those who caught the plague died." One doctor, a man named Francesco, who served as health officer in Venice for 17 years, was given an annual stipend of 25 gold ducats for staying in the city during the Black Death "when nearly all physicians withdrew on account of fear and terror." When asked why he didn't flee, Francesco responded, "I would rather die here than live elsewhere."

In the city of Orvieto the physician hired by the city before the plague received 25 lira a year, when he was paid at all. After the plague this same physician was offered a salary of 200 lira a year plus exemption from all city taxes. This reward was not surprising, as the existing evidence indicates that only one of every eight physicians lived through the Black Death. Their colleagues, the surgeons and barbers, fared even worse. In the French city of Perpignan, only 2 of the 18 surgeons and barbers survived.

Physicians in the medieval period were trained by the Catholic Church. However, the central mission of the Church was not medicine, but contemplation of God. Because of this, there was a struggle between the ancient Hippocratic and Galenic rational approaches to medicine and the Church's interest in seeing illness as a punishment for sin. Most physicians continued to use the traditions of Hippocrates and Galen; however, the influence of religion in the lives of most common people was strong, and physicians did not want to insult those beliefs. Complicating matters was the fact that physicians had only limited knowledge and tools. Microscopes would not be in use until 1600 and would not be powerful until 1870. This meant that there was no understanding of the "microscopic" elements of the world, including bacteria. Autopsies were allowed in Italy after 1316, but physicians and surgeons were not sure that seeing the inside of the body was helpful. After all, they had the writings of Galen from 1,000 years before. Basically they trusted that he had gotten it right.

Disaster in
the Cities

The Black Death entered Genoa through the city's busy harbor, shown here. When the Genoese discovered that sailors were dying of plague, they forced the men back onto their ships and drove them away with flaming arrows. Unfortunately, the Black Death had already gained a foothold in the Italian city.

5

When Genoa's city leaders discovered that sailors were dying of plague, they ordered the men back onto the ships and drove them from shore. The healthy sailors, unwilling to join their sick crewmates, had to be forced. The Genoese used burning arrows and other weapons of war to prevent the ships from returning to harbor. Unfortunately, they reacted too late, and plague plunged deep into the city.

Genoa's city leaders weren't alone in their delayed reaction. Two hundred miles away, in the Italian cities of Venice and Florence, plague would strike with even greater ferocity. Both cities, like Genoa, were great trading powers, and Venice's ties to shipping would make it one of the first cities to be afflicted with the plague.

By March 20, 1348, the leader of the Venetian Republic, Doge Andrea

Dandolo, was concerned enough to appoint a panel of three noblemen to determine how to halt the spread of plague in the city. As in many other cities, the recommendations included special burial places for victims. Because Venice is built on more than 100 tiny islands connected by canals, special barges were assigned the job of collecting the dead. The Venetians refused to allow new people to enter their city, and ships that tried to evade the rules were threatened with burning. However, these measures didn't prevent the spread of the disease. During the worst of the plague it is said that 600 Venetians died every day. Although the death rate could not have continued this high for very long without killing the entire population, such a large number is not unbelievable at the height of the outbreak.

When the plague arrived in Florence, the city fathers established a "committee of eight" to oversee control of the disease. This committee was given near dictatorial power—an indication of the extent of the city leaders' concern, for the great cities of Italy had for centuries been proud of the liberties promised to their citizens. Unfortunately in Florence, as in Venice, the strict emergency rules put in place regarding who could enter and leave the city and about the burial of the dead did not halt the spread of the plague. In fact, the death rate in Florence, one of the hardest-hit cities in all of Europe, soon climbed so high that not enough people remained to remove the bodies to cemeteries.

It is difficult to tell from the surviving records exactly how many people were living in Florence before the plague. Certainly, it was one of the most prosperous of the Italian cities, which in general were larger than those of northern Europe. Based on estimates putting Florence's preplague population at just under 100,000, historians believe that the Black Death claimed up to

A distraught mother laments the death of her young daughter in this painting depicting the plague in Florence. One of the hardest-hit cities in all of Europe, Florence lost more than half its population—up to 65,000 people—in just six months.

65,000 victims in the six months that it raged within the city walls.

Giovanni Boccaccio, a citizen of Florence, left one of the best firsthand accounts of life during the plague. At the height of the plague Boccaccio wrote: "many died daily or nightly in the public streets; so many others, who died at home, the departure was hardly observed by their neighbors, until the stench of their putrefying bodies carry the tidings; and what with their corpses and the corpses of others who died on every hand the whole place was a sepulchre."

Florence was typical of a plague city. So many people died, friends and neighbors stopped attending the funerals. The victims were simply carried off stacked several to a bier on the shoulders of men hired to do the odious work. Or, even less dignified, the bodies were stacked in

THE BLACK DEATH IN FICTION: BOCCACCIO'S *DECAMERON*

Giovanni Boccaccio (1313–1375) lived in Florence before and after the Black Death. Drawing on his experiences during the plague, he wrote the *Decameron,* the story of seven young women and three young men who flee the stricken city for the countryside. In the preface to the work, Boccaccio describes a city in the grip of fear, a city where death is so common that a corpse could go unnoticed on the street. He tells of parents abandoning their children and of sickness transmitted by speaking with, touching, or even seeing someone who was already ill. In the *Decameron* the 10 young people leave for the countryside to reduce their chances of getting the plague. They stay in the country for 10 days (the name of the book comes from the Greek *deka hererai,* meaning "10 days"), and on each day a different member of the party has to tell a story for the amusement of the others. The *Decameron* has been called a profound expression of the love of life because Boccaccio was living through the greatest of horrors when he wrote it, yet the tale is filled only with stories of fun and jest and laughter. The quality of his writing, combined with his moral attitude, has earned Boccaccio a place among the greatest Italian writers.

carts. Often one bier would carry an entire family. People were no longer buried in sacred ground or churchyards; instead hastily dug trenches sufficed. Boccaccio describes the sight of the trenches: "they laid the corpses as they arrived by hundreds at a time, piling them up as merchandise is stowed in the hold of a ship, tier upon tier, each covered with a little earth, until the trench would hold no more."

In some Italian cities, leaders took decisive and forceful action to avoid the repetition of scenes like this in their hometowns. The first cases of plague discovered in Milan involved the occupants of three houses. The city leaders immediately ordered that the houses be sealed with all occupants—healthy and sick—inside. Naturally, all of the occupants of these houses died. Whether from this action or for other unknown reasons, Milan was the least affected of the large Italian cities.

Another Italian town, Pistoia, left detailed records of the activities of the city council during the plague. These records give a clear sense of the progression of events. They also show how little was known about the spread of plague and how little a city could do to prevent it. In Pistoia, on May 2, 1348, the city council noted that cases of plague had appeared in the town's vicinity. Deciding to take action, the council dictated nine pages of regulations that were intended to protect the city. Central to these were restrictions on travel. No one was to visit the neighboring states of Pisa or Lucca, where plague was rampant. People who had gone to those states before the new regulations took effect were forbidden to come back. The importation of goods, including linen and wool, was forbidden no matter what the source. There was a specific ban on bringing corpses into the city. Food markets, which were largely outdoors, were placed under strict council supervision in a general effort to control rot and spoilage. Attendance at funerals—even of people who had died of causes other than the plague—was restricted to family members. Strict rules were established for the places where burials could occur, as well as for the depth of the graves. It was clear in all of these new regulations that the city council was concerned about contact with materials that might carry plague. But the regulations also indicate that the council members believed the arrival of plague inevitable—and because of this were more concerned about minimizing its spread within the city walls and managing the social upheaval it might create. For example, among the last set of regulations enacted was one that prohibited the ringing of bells at funerals and another that prohibited the announcement of death by the town criers or trumpeters. Evidently the council members felt that news of too many deaths might disturb those who were ill and be bad for city morale.

Twenty-one days later, on May 23, 1348, a second set of ordinances was set in place. By now the plague was firmly established within the city walls and restrictions on travel were useless. However, while restrictions on travel were overturned, the regulations for the supervision of markets were strengthened. A further modification of the rules was made on June 4. This change concerned funerals. The number of dead was becoming a problem, and 16 men from each part of town were selected as official gravediggers.

A final reworking of the emergency regulations came on June 13, a total of 42 days after the initial regulations had been put in place. This provides one of the few examples of differences being made between the rich and the poor in the fight for survival against the plague. The final plague ordinance in Pistoia allowed members of the cavalry, who defended the city walls, to pay a substitute to perform their duties. The cavalry, which was composed mostly of wealthier citizens, could thus stay at home to escape the disease.

In contrast to Pistoia, where city councilmen took every precaution to prevent the plague from entering the city, the small town of Orvieto in Italy did nothing. Orvieto had around 12,000 citizens and was prosperous in the spring of 1348. For months the plague had raged in cities and towns nearby, but no official mention of it is made in council minutes. Some historians speculate that the citizens of Orvieto did nothing because they hoped the plague would pass them by if they ignored it. Others believe that a sense of inevitability might have prevailed, with citizens feeling that any precautions would be useless. In fact, there was probably little the city could have done. Orvieto had only one doctor and one surgeon, neither of whom was equipped to cope with the disease. In addition, Orvieto had another problem common to medieval towns: terrible public hygiene. Laws of the period are filled with warnings against raising goats and pigs in city streets, tanning skins in the heat of midday, and throwing trash and waste from windows. The laws indicate concern with the problem, but the continual updating of the laws indicates that the problem was never resolved. Because of this one of the plague's natural allies, filth, was everywhere.

In April of 1348 the plague arrived in Orvieto. In early June a "council of seven" was elected to govern the city. By July 23, two of the council members were dead, and three more had died by August 7. Another was dead by August 21. The seventh member fell ill but recovered. The city's most important religious ceremony, the procession of the Assumption, normally held on August 15, was canceled. However, the plague disappeared as abruptly as it had arrived, and by the end of August the city council was meeting again. Shops were reopened, and three new public notaries and two new gatekeepers were appointed

(continued on page 78)

THE MEDIEVAL HOSPITAL

The hospital as an institution providing specialized medical care developed in the early medieval period. Constantinople, in the Byzantine Empire, boasted one of the earliest known hospitals. The Muslim world also had some renowned examples, the best known of which were in Baghdad, Damascus, and Cairo. Baghdad's first hospital dated to the ninth century. At the combination hospital and medical school in Damascus, rooms were so elegant and the library so extensive that healthy people feigned illness to enjoy the accommodations. In the 12th century, the Pantokrator hospital in Constantinople had space for 50 patients—38 men and 12 women—and was staffed by 47 people, including physicians and surgeons. Beyond this there is very little precise information regarding the earliest hospitals.

By the 12th and 13th centuries, when the plague swept through Europe, many cities and towns had at least one hospital. Varying in size from large (hundreds of beds) to small (a half-dozen beds), they were funded by private donors, city governments, and the Catholic Church. Typically their patients came from the lower classes because wealthy people could afford to summon physicians to their homes. The physicians who worked in hospitals were paid an annual salary.

Typically, large city hospitals were entered from the street through a large door that would also allow carts and horses into the central courtyard. Surrounding the courtyard were all of the hospital facilities. There would be a large open room for the patients, an apothecary where drugs and herbs were kept, kitchens, laundries, dormitories for the nuns who served as nurses, and, of course, a chapel for prayer. Sometimes the chapel was one end of the large room where the patients slept, so that even bedridden patients could hear Mass and prayers. Most hospitals had another medium-sized room for the care of infectious patients, including plague victims. The largest hospitals had separate rooms for different types of ailments, including fevers, eye conditions, diarrhea, wounds, and female disorders. The only patients not treated at regular hospitals were lepers, who were unwelcome in smaller towns and restricted to special hospitals in larger ones.

In medieval hospitals special attention was paid to cleanliness. Each patient would have a bed, a real luxury in the Middle Ages, surrounded by a heavy curtain. Often the staff was composed of nuns, who would keep patients clean, give them food, and administer herbal remedies. One large hospital in Milan

A medieval hospital, Italy. By the time plague swept through Europe in the 14th century, many cities and towns had at least one hospital.

boasted three physicians. The city of Florence was proud of its 15 hospitals.

During times of plague the room reserved for infectious patients would fill quickly. A chronicler in Paris during the Black Death observed that "so great was the mortality that for a long time more than 500 corpses were carted daily to the churchyard of St. Innocent to be buried." Historians have proposed that this number was a misprint for 50. Even so, this is a large number. William of Nangis said, "Those holy sisters, having no fear of death, tended the sick with all sweetness and humility, putting all honour behind their back." The loyalty of these "sweet sisters" is especially noteworthy because in Paris, as in other cities, the general rule was save oneself.

(continued from page 75)

to replace those who had died, indicating that the city was returning to business as usual. Although more than 50 percent of its citizens had died, Orvieto would survive, and to visitors would appear largely unchanged.

This was not the case in the Italian city of Siena. When plague struck there, work was under way on what the city hoped would be the greatest cathedral in the Christian world. But the workmen died and money for the project was used for other, more urgent, needs. One resident wrote that "father abandoned child; wife, husband; one brother, another; for this illness seemed to strike through the breath and the sight. And so they died. And no one could be found to bury the dead for money or for friendship. . . . And I, Agnolo di Tura, called the Fat, buried my five children with my own hands, and so did many others likewise. And there were also many dead throughout the city who were so sparsely covered with earth that the dogs dragged them forth and devoured their bodies."

Historians believe that of an original population of nearly 50,000, only a few thousand remained in Siena after the Black Death had departed. The city would never be the same. Despite tax incentives to encourage people to move to the city, Siena never fully recovered its preplague population.

An exceptional number of Sienese clergy died in the plague—so many, in fact, that some positions that had formerly been reserved for monks and priests were given to other citizens. Despite this loss of manpower, the Catholic Church benefited financially. Frightened citizens made huge donations in return for special prayers and protection, and the wills of many of the dead left property to the Church as well. In fact, the Church received so much through the combination of

inheritance and gifts that in October 1348 the city suspended all annual appropriations to religious persons and institutions for two years. It was not only the Church that benefited indirectly from the plague. The city itself received title to a fair amount of land from families in which no heirs were left alive. The remaining members of the traditional oligarchy, or ruling class, gained greater strength as well. Their fortunes were increased by inheritance from dead relatives and by the fact that there were fewer people left to share the wealth.

Members of the clergy comfort and pray for a plague victim. Though priests generally had the means to flee the Black Death, records show that an exceptional number died, indicating that most chose to stay with their flocks.

Vos Creditis, als eine fabel,
quod scribitur vom Doctor schnabel,
der fugit die Contagion
et aufert seinen Lohn darvon.
Cadavera sucht er zu frysten
gleich wie der Corvus auf der Misten.
Ah Credite, ziehet nicht dort hin
dann Romæ regnat die Pestin.

Quis non deberet sehr erschrecken
für seiner Virgul oder stecken,
quä loquitur, als wär er stumm
und deutet sein Consilium
wie mancher Credit ohne zweiffel
das ihm tentir ein schwarzen Teuffel
Marsupium heyst seine Höll
und aurum die geholte seel

J. Columbina ad vivum delineavit

Paulus Fürst Excudit

No Escape

On August 19, 1349, Thomas Bradwardine landed at the English port of Dover. He was returning from Avignon in France where he had received the pope's blessing for his consecration as arch-bishop of Canterbury, the top position in the Roman Catholic Church in England. At 59 years of age the clergyman and former Oxford University academic was considered an elder statesman of the Church. Upon his arrival in Dover, he met with his king, Edward III. Two days later, on August 21, Bradwardine went to Rochester to the palace of the bishop of that diocese. The next morning he developed a high fever. Despite the fact that plague had been in England for the past year, no one was worried. They thought that the fever was the result of Bradwardine's long journey and his age. That evening the archbishop developed buboes on his groin and armpits. The transition from fever to full-blown plague was swift—Bradwardine died five days later. He had probably contracted the disease as the result of a fleabite while on board the ship.

Because of his status as the most important man in the church in England, Bradwardine's body was carried the 20 miles to Canterbury, where he was buried in Canterbury Cathedral.

Plague had inspired such fear of its victims' bodies that few others were given this attention. Certainly those who lived in the surrounding villages were not treated with the same respect.

It's not clear exactly when plague entered the island country of England. It probably arrived by ship between mid-June and August of 1348. Some historians believe that the port of entry was Melcombe Regis and that the carrier was a ship from the French port of Calais. It's even more difficult to tell exactly how the plague spread across the country. Few firsthand accounts, like those found in Italy, survive. What little is known historians have pieced together from a few letters, Church documents, and census and tax records.

What is clear is that as village after village was struck, the population decreased rapidly. English villages, where 90 percent of the population lived, were the heart of the country.

By January 1349 the bishop of Bath and Wells, Ralph of Shrewsbury, was so concerned by the death of large numbers of his priests that he circulated a letter with emergency instructions. In his letter Shrewsbury expressed his regret that so many priests were dead and that there was no one left to take care of the needs of the people. Shrewsbury suggested that for the "salvation of souls," confession of sins could be made to anyone, including women. Shrewsbury's next concession was even more startling. He stated that if no priest were available, then the sacrament of extreme unction, the ritual that prepared the soul for death, could be skipped. Instead, he said, "faith must suffice."

Cynics have observed that Shrewsbury did not venture from his winter home in the remote village of Wiveliscombe. But others have countered that the bishop may have seen the wisdom in protecting himself so that he could take care of the business of the Church. Shrewsbury did receive a stream of visitors on official Church business, and he didn't avoid contact with local plague victims. Across his diocese, the evidence suggests that priests tended to their flocks and as a result died in great numbers. There were nine new appointments to office in the diocese in the month of November 1348. In December there were 32, followed by 47 in January 1349. The next months proved just as deadly, with 43 new appointments in February, 36 in March, and 40 in April. Finally the plague seems to have left the area; only 21 new appointments were made in May, and just 7 in June. The confusion that surrounded all activities, evident in the emergency measures Shrewsbury authorized, is also revealed by a legal document he had prepared. The document protected him in case he acted too hastily and appointed a new priest to an office not yet vacated.

On July 28, 1348, Archbishop Zouche of York, England—alarmed by news of the death toll on the Continent—sent a letter to the priests in his diocese. He warned that man's never-ending battle with the wickedness of the world was about to become more intense with the arrival of pestilence. The archbishop believed that his people would be strengthened if they engaged in an "outpouring of spiritual grace in their time of infirmity." To avert the plague the archbishop recommended prayer.

Although talk of prayer and God's grace was important on one level, on another level it could not eliminate the fear that engulfed the English countryside. A typical village in the south of England, which might consist of 30 or so families and about 150 people, was quite isolated. Typically, no more than a footpath would link the village with a main road—to London perhaps—and few, if any, of the villagers would ever have visited a city. In fact, many would never have traveled outside their own village. Some families may have been among the freemen who merely paid rent to the local lord, but in the 14th century many would still have been serfs—peasants who were legally bound to the lord and to the land they cultivated on his behalf. Some cloth and an occasional manufactured item might find their way into an English village, but for the most part little trade was conducted with the outside world. The most important people were the steward of the lord and the priest of the local church.

A village family slept on the mud floor of their cottage on rough beds made of handfuls of straw. In good years they drank cider or beer; in bad they contented themselves with water drawn from a stream or well.

Occasionally strangers might pass through a village on their way to London or another town, perhaps stopping to ask the locals for directions, to rest their horses, or to get something to eat. During the time of the Black Death, such a visit could bring ruin to an isolated village if the strangers had been infected with the disease.

This is the way it might have unfolded. Eight hours or so after coming into contact with the travelers, villagers would have felt tired. The next morning they would have been feverish. Their arms and legs would have hurt and they would have had a blinding headache. By late afternoon they may well have been unable to stand. Frightened, families would probably have summoned the priest for help. Ideally, the priest would have arrived with the personal physician of the local lord, who would want to be apprised if plague had entered his holdings so that he could leave.

Many physicians wore elaborate layers of clothing and a mask to keep diseased air from their bodies. The plague mask had a long, pointed nose, which held vinegar to ward off disease and perfumes to prevent the physician from smelling the stench of open buboes. One look at the strange sight must have terrified many a common peasant sick in his bed.

Many victims passed into a delirious sleep before death. In their confused state they would have had a hard time understanding the bizarre behavior of the living. In some villages, the first case of plague would signal the healthy residents to open all of their casks of cider and wine. Certain that they would drop dead at any moment and determined to spend their final minutes having fun, they drank, danced, and sang. In many cases the entire village *would* eventually become sick. Victims would drop dead and lay where they fell, a few in the streets, most in their beds. Those who were able might run into the fields and woods surrounding the village in a final, desperate attempt to save themselves.

Approximately half of the people living in England died in the plague. Many towns and villages were utterly destroyed. More than 150 years would pass before the population in some towns again reached its pre–Black Death numbers. At least 15 towns permanently ceased to exist.

In many villages, residents consumed their stores of wine and cider, sang, and danced at the first sign of plague in their midst. Convinced that they would all die, they wanted to enjoy their final moments.

Monasteries, which were really villages unto themselves, suffered similar fates. At the Abbey of Meaux the monks believed they had been warned. On the Friday before Passion Sunday, they had been shaken by an earthquake. This omen was followed by the birth and death of Siamese twins in the nearby village. Because of these events the monks knew that disaster was coming. On August 12, 1349, the abbot and five monks died. The prior, the cellarer, the bursar, and 17 other monks died in the succeeding days. After the plague had passed, only 10 of the original 50 members of the community were still alive.

Brother John Clyn, a member of the Order of Friars Minor at the convent of Kilkenny, Ireland, kept a journal in which he recorded the coming of the plague. He wrote, he said, so that if anyone survived, that person could carry on the work John had begun. Thousands of pilgrims, John said, flocked to the great religious centers during the plague, and the Black Death claimed most of their lives anyway. In Dublin alone, according to the friar, between the beginning of August and Christmas 1349, as many as 14,000 people died. Later someone else added to John Clyn's text, "Here it seems that the author died."

For many surviving peasants like the ones pictured here, the Black Death ultimately brought a better way of life. Because of the severe labor shortage caused by the plague, peasants who were formerly bound to the land they worked—and the lord who owned it—could now move away in search of higher wages and better working conditions.

Aftermath

The Black Death changed Europe in profound ways. Indeed, some historians maintain that the plague led to the emergence of a whole new way of thinking about humanity and our place in the world—in short, to the modern man and woman. Other historians would not go quite that far. But everyone agrees that after the tremendous decline in population, life in late medieval Europe was radically different.

Survivors of the plague had to take stock of the situation. Many of them had lost their entire families. Surviving children had a particularly difficult time, because they were often without resources to take care of themselves. Food prices had risen sharply because so many of the peasants who grew the crops were dead. Merchants didn't need to hire help; they had no clients left to buy their goods. Even the famous Italian banks were in trouble.

On the other hand, all across Europe some survivors found themselves with large inheritances. Often, money that would have been parceled out among many children went to the one family member left, and that person would suddenly be very well off. In many cases, a distant relative suddenly inherited an estate that had been carefully managed for generations. Sometimes no living relative survived to inherit the property. Records from the village of Farnham in England illustrate just how frequently this happened. When property was inherited in a lord's domain, the lord collected a fine from the person to whom the property passed. In Farnham in 1350, so many people died that the inheritance fine was forfeited 40 times because there was no one left to inherit the property.

In England, the remaining peasants in some small villages demanded better tax rates from the local lords. When the lords refused, the peasants left. In a move often called "voting with their feet" the peasants, who were legally obligated to live on the land and pay taxes to the lord, simply walked away in search of a better situation. They did not have to travel far before they found lords whose peasants had died and who were desperate for someone to farm their land. Indeed, the lords were so desperate that they overlooked the fact that these peasants had fled another lord's domain. This would never have happened before the plague. Only a severe shortage of labor that threatened the food supply made such lawlessness acceptable.

By 1351, as the plague was ending, the English Parliament already understood the problems that were being created by the loss of labor. Wages had escalated during the plague years because the number of laborers had sharply decreased and that made their time more valuable. In Cuxham, England, a ploughman was paid two shillings per year before the plague. The same ploughman earned 7 shillings in 1349–1350 and more than 10 shillings in 1350–1351. Similar increases happened in other fields of labor.

At the same time, the value of goods being sold, from animals to wool, fell because there was less demand. This meant that the local lord was paying his laborers more while he was making less from the sale of their goods at market. Parliament responded with the Statute of Laborers, an attempt to freeze wages at pre–Black Death levels. The peasants, who understood how valuable their work was and who had grown accustomed to having more money in their pockets, chafed at this legislation. A silent struggle continued until 1381, when, 30 years after the plague, the peasants revolted. They killed the archbishop of Canterbury, then saw their own leader killed at Smithfield. The English peasants were not alone, however. All across Europe in the years following the Black Death, laborers fought for their rights.

Cities also learned from their experiences during the plague. In Venice ships coming from possibly infected areas had to stay across the Adriatic Sea in Ragusa for 30 days (later increased to 40 days) to demonstrate that they were not carrying disease. The modern term *quarantine* derives from this waiting period, from the Italian word *quaranta,* meaning "forty."

The plague also decreased the number of skilled masons available to work on buildings. Those who lived were overworked and used less complicated techniques, either to save time or because they were not as well trained as their predecessors. Because of this, some critics feel that the great cathedrals built after the plague are inferior to those built before. But perhaps they were simply different in style as a result of the arrival of a new generation of masons.

THE *DANSE MACABRE*

The *Danse Macabre,* or Dance of Death, was first depicted around 1485 in Paris in the Church of the Holy Innocents. More than 100 years after the Black Death, this artistic representation of life became increasingly popular. In the Dance of Death naked, rotting corpses dance with great animation before the living. The living, in clothing that represents different social orders, are immobile, surprised by death but resigned to their fate. This view of life and the world was one of the important long-term results of the plague.

A woodcut print depicting the Danse Macabre, *or Dance of Death.*

The plague also brought tremendous change to the Catholic Church. Approximately half of the parish priests had died. In England the Church, in an effort to recruit new priests quickly, virtually ignored the steps normally required for ordination. Before the plague new members of the priesthood were usually young and educated, and—in accordance with church rules—had never been married. After the plague, many men who had lost their wives to the disease became priests. One man in the diocese of Bath and Wells was admitted even though his wife was still living. The bishop of Norwich obtained permission from the pope to allow 60 clerks under the age of 21 to hold rectories. He asked for this permission based on the grounds that someone—anyone—serving as parish priest was better than no one. This is not to say that these men were less devout than their predecessors. However, some of the older clergy did object. A man named Knighton, for example, complained that the new priests were uneducated and greedy. "A very great multitude of men whose wives had died of the pestilence flocked to Holy Orders of whom many were illiterate. . . . A man could scarcely get a chaplain to undertake any church for less than £10 or ten marks." Knighton put this increase in perspective: before the plague, he observed, there had been plenty of priests who were paid only two marks and daily bread.

Although the priesthood was hit hard by the plague, those who lived in monasteries were even worse off. In England before the plague there were approximately 17,500 monks, nuns, and friars. About half of these religious people died during the two years the plague raged. The monasteries never returned to their former numbers, for several reasons. First, the panic of the plague changed the pattern of donation to the church, leaving monasteries with a smaller share than before. Second, there was an increase in other economic opportunities after the plague. Before the plague the Church had offered the best way of advancement for all members of society. After the plague people were able to leave jobs they didn't like just as peasants left land they didn't like for better prospects. A third problem was the decrease in tithes paid by local people. With fewer people left to support the Church, less money was tithed. Some monasteries, unable to cope with the change, slipped into debt. A well-known Franciscan monk put it this way: "It was because of [the Black Death] that the monastic Orders . . . began to decline. Discipline became slack and faith weakened, both because of the loss of their most eminent members and the relaxation of rules that ensued as a result of these calamities. It was in vain to look to the young men who had been received without proper selection and training to bring about a reform since they thought more about filling up the empty houses than about restoring the lost sense of authority."

At the same time, the Church flourished in other ways. Many churches were built across Europe as the result of money donated or bequeathed during the plague. The magnificent cathedral of Milan is the most dramatic example of this flurry of building, but many village churches were also built in Italy, England, and France between 1350 and 1375. In Italy nearly 50 new religious holidays were created. This was inspired by relief at the end of the plague and the belief that unless given more attention, the Almighty might unleash another disaster. And, despite the tremendous death toll, the total number of pilgrims making the holy journey to Rome did not decrease. This meant that a higher percentage of the population was undertaking the pilgrimage.

Although the plague caused taxes to rise and peasants

to revolt, it also affected people on a more personal level. After the plague, life seemed more valuable. People wanted to celebrate. There was also an increased sense of individuality and independence. With this came a new appreciation for variety. All told, somewhere between one-third to one-half of the people of Europe died in the years of the Black Death. The shock of such devastating horror was followed by years of rebuilding. With fewer people, living conditions altered, jobs changed, villages ceased to exist, and manor houses remained empty—but the celebration of life overcame the realization that life was precarious. Some historians have suggested that it was this long-term impact of the Black Death that gave the Renaissance in Europe its creative energy.

Chronology

1333   A series of natural disasters in the Far East begins (earthquakes, floods, drought, famine, and swarms of locusts)

1346   Stories reach Europe about a plague far to the east (India and China); Genoese escape siege of Caffa, sail to Mediterranean carrying the Black Death

1347   Plague arrives in Constantinople (modern Istanbul, Turkey), spreads along Turkey on the Mediterranean coast; by October it has reached Sicily

1348   *January:* Plague arrives in Genoa and Venice

   February: Plague arrives in Pisa, from where it spreads to central and northern Italy

   April: Plague strikes Florence; inspires Boccaccio's *Decameron*

   June: Plague has spread across all of Italy, half of Spain, and across France almost to the northern coast on a line stretching through modern Switzerland

   December: Plague has traveled farther north across Europe, crossed the English Channel to strike Weymouth in the region of Dorset in southwest Britain; plague stretches across the lower part of modern Germany

1349   *June:* Plague has reached the Scottish highlands of Britain, also entered the eastern half of Ireland

   December: All of England and Ireland are affected; plague has spread throughout northern Europe, crossed the North and Baltic Seas to Scandinavia

1351   Plague has virtually ended in Europe; Flagellants disperse in most areas

1380s   Peasant uprisings in Europe occur as a result of economic problems worsened by the plague

Further Reading

Altman, Linda Jacobs. *Plague and Pestilence: A History of Infectious Disease*. Springfield, N.J.: Enslow, 1998.

Cantor, Norman F. *In the Wake of the Plague*. New York: Free Press, 2001.

Giblin, James Cross. *When Plague Strikes: The Black Death, Smallpox, AIDS*. New York: HarperCollins, 1995.

Nardo, Don, ed. *The Black Death*. San Diego: Greenhaven, 1999.

Ricker, John, and John Saywell. *The Emergence of Europe*. Evanston, Ill.: McDougal, Littell, 1976.

Ziegler, Philip. *The Black Death*. Phoenix Mill, UK: Alan Sutton, 1991.

Index

Africa, plague in, 52
Alfonso of Córdoba, 61
Aloe, as treatment, 63
Asia, plague in, 52
Astrology, 63
Atra mors, 28

Barbers, 60, 66-67
Barna Ciuriani,
    Valorino de, 52
Becchini, 26
Benefices, 53
Black Death
    accounts of, 13-14, 24-25,
        29-32, 47, 72, 78, 87
    and aftermath, 89-91,
        93-95
    and analysis of bones of
        victims of, 11-14, 15
    and astrology, 63
    bad-air theories of,
        60-61, 62, 63
    and bathing, 62
    behavior of women as
        cause of, 57-58
    and burial customs,
        26, 72-73, 74
    in cities, 66, 69-70,
        72-74, 78-79, 91
    and collection of
        dead, 26, 70, 72-73
    deaths from, 27, 52,
        53, 70, 72, 78, 85,
        87, 90, 95
    descriptions, 12, 25,
        29-32, 38-39, 41-42,
        44-46, 84-85

and endemic periods,
    38-39
end of, 90
and epidemic periods,
    38-39, 45
fear associated with,
    22, 31-32
and first recorded
    outbreak of, 39
and fleas, 24, 27-28,
    41-44, 45, 46
and flight from cities,
    22, 27
as God's punishment,
    17, 38, 52, 54, 57. *See
    also* Catholic Church
and lack of pattern of,
    52
and lawlessness, 26,
    53, 90
and masons, 91
in monasteries, 86-87,
    93-94
and mortality rate,
    45-46
and name given to
    epidemic, 28-29, 46
and natural disasters
    in Far East, 50-52
origin of, 21-22, 24-25,
    39, 41, 82
and pandemics, 39, 41
path of, 17-19, 23
and peasant uprisings,
    90-91
and poisonous cloud,
    25, 32, 50-52, 60-61

and quarantining
    houses, 62
and quarantining
    ships, 91
and rats, 41, 42-44
spread of, 17-19, 21-25,
    27-28, 32-33, 35-37,
    41-46, 82
stories about origin
    of, 22, 24-25
survivors of, 89-90
and three types of
    plague, 44-46
transmission of, 41-44,
    46
treatment of, 62-64,
    66
and unhealthful
    conditions, 15-17,
    75
and weather, 42, 46
and wills, 54, 78-79
See also Catholic
    Church; England,
    plague in; Italy,
    plague in; Physi-
    cians; Priests
Boccaccio, Giovanni,
    29, 30, 72
Bordeaux, plague in,
    36-38
Bradwardine, Thomas,
    81-82
Brethren of the Cross.
    See Flagellants
Buboes, 12, 28, 29, 30,
    32, 44

Index

Index

Picture Credits

TRACEE DE HAHN is a freelance writer living in Lexington, Kentucky. In addition to her undergraduate degree in architecture, she holds a master's degree in European history. She is also the author of *The Blizzard of 1888* in this series.

JILL McCAFFREY has served for four years as national chairman of the Armed Forces Emergency Services of the American Red Cross. Ms. McCaffrey also serves on the board of directors for Knollwood—the Army Distaff Hall. The former Jill Ann Faulkner, a Massachusetts native, is the wife of Barry R. McCaffrey, who served in President Bill Clinton's cabinet as director of the White House Office of National Drug Control Policy. The McCaffreys are the parents of three grown children: Sean, a major in the U.S. Army; Tara, an intensive care nurse and captain in the National Guard; and Amy, a seventh grade teacher. The McCaffreys also have two grandchildren, Michael and Jack.